Editor - Zachary Rau
Contributing Editor - Robert Langhorn
Graphic Designer and Letterer - Tomás Montalvo-Lagos
Cover Designer - Jorge Negrete
Graphic Artists - Anna Kernbaum, John Lo, Louis Csontos and Monalisa J. de Asis

Digital Imaging Manager - Chris Buford
Production Managers - Jennifer Miller and Mutsumi Miyazaki
Senior Designer - Anna Kernbaum
Senior Editor - Elizabeth Hurchalla
Managing Editor - Lindsey Johnston
VP of Production - Ron Klamert
Publisher & Editor in Chief - Mike Kiley
President & C.O.O. - John Parker
C.E.O. - Stuart Levy

E-mail: info@TOKYOPOP.com
Come visit us online at www.TOKYOPOP.com

A ⊙ TOKYOPOP® Cine-Manga® Book
TOKYOPOP Inc.
5900 Wilshire Blvd., Suite 2000
Los Angeles, CA 90036

Avatar: The Last Airbender Volume 1

ISBN: 1-59532-891-2

First TOKYOPOP® printing: February 2006

10 9 8 7 6 5 4 3 2 1

Printed in Canada

NICKELODEON

降击神通

AVATAR

THE LAST AIRBENDER

CREATED BY
MICHAEL DANTE DiMARTINO &
BRYAN KONIETZKO

NICKELODEON

AVATAR

THE LAST AIRBENDER.

AANG –
THE LAST OF THE
AIRBENDERS.

UNCLE IROH –
PRINCE ZUKO'S
GUARDIAN.

PRINCE ZUKO –
A MEMBER OF THE FIRE NATION
AND THE OLDEST SON OF THE
FIRE LORD, OZAI. HE HAS BEEN
BANISHED BY HIS FATHER
AND CAN ONLY RETURN HOME
WHEN HE CAPTURES THE AVATAR,
DEAD OR ALIVE.

NICKELODEON

降去神通

AVATAR

THE LAST AIRBENDER

VOL.1 CONTENTS

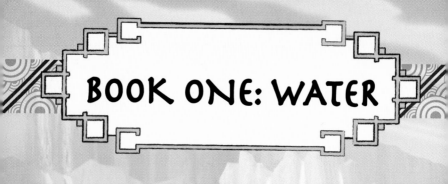

BOOK ONE: WATER

THE BOY IN THE ICEBERG

WRITTEN BY
MICHAEL DANTE DIMARTINO
& BRYAN KONIETZKO

ADDITIONAL WRITING BY
AARON EHASZ, PETER GOLDFINGER
AND JOSH STOLBERG

SO, DO YOU GUYS LIVE AROUND HERE?

DON'T ANSWER THAT, KATARA! DID YOU SEE THAT CRAZY BOLT OF LIGHT? HE WAS PROBABLY TRYING TO SIGNAL THE FIRE NAVY!

YEAH, I'M SURE HE'S A SPY FOR THE FIRE NAVY...YOU CAN TELL BY THE LOOK IN HIS EYE.

.....

THWUMP...

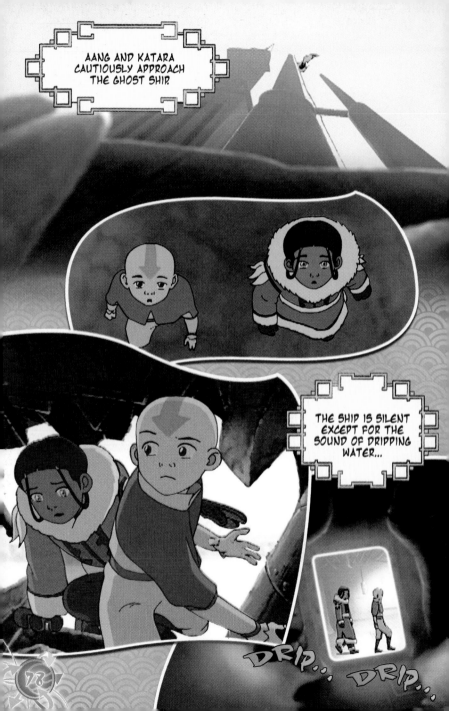

AANG AND KATARA CAUTIOUSLY APPROACH THE GHOST SHIP

THE SHIP IS SILENT EXCEPT FOR THE SOUND OF DRIPPING WATER...

DRIP... DRIP...

HISSSSS!!

SUDDENLY, THERE IS A HIGH-PITCHED SCREAMING NOISE AS THE SHIP'S DEFENSE SYSTEMS LAUNCH A SIGNAL FLARE THAT EXPLODES HIGH ABOVE THE ICY PLAIN.

SKEEEEEEEE!!

UH-OH....

THE FOUR NATIONS

群雄四分

WATER

EARTH

FIRE

AIR

天下一匡

WATER TRIBES

MEMBERS OF THE WATER TRIBES OF THE NORTH AND SOUTH POLE HAVE THE ABILITY TO BEND WATER, ALTHOUGH THE NORTH POLE HAS MANY MORE WATERBENDERS. KATARA IS THE ONLY KNOWN PERSON WITH WATERBENDING SKILL IN THE SOUTHERN TRIBE. SINCE THE OUTBREAK OF WAR WITH THE FIRE NATION, THE TWO TRIBES HAVE NOT HAD CONTACT. THE WATER TRIBES ARE CLOSELY ASSOCIATED WITH WINTER.

A WATERBENDER'S POWERS ARE STRENGTHENED BY THE MOON'S CYCLES AND THE RAIN. THEY CANNOT CONJURE WATER OUT OF THIN AIR, THERE MUST BE WATER AROUND THEM. IT IS POSSIBLE, THOUGH, FOR WATERBENDERS TO MANIPULATE MOISTURE IN THE AIR. WATERBENDING IS A DEFENSIVE ART WITH THE INTENTION OF CONTROLLING THE OPPONENT, NOT HARMING HIM. WATERBENDERS CAN ENCASE THEIR OPPONENTS IN BLOCKS OR THEY CAN ESCAPE BY CREATING A SHEET OF STEAM.

NOT EVERYBODY HAS THE ABILITY TO BEND. THIS IS TRUE OF ALL THE NATIONS WITH THE ONE EXCEPTION BEING THE AIR NOMADS, WHO ARE ALL AIRBENDERS. IN THE OTHER NATIONS, BENDERS MAKE UP ONLY A SMALL PERCENTAGE OF THE PEOPLE. MEMBERS OF THE WATER TRIBE WHO DO NOT POSSESS BENDING SKILLS USE BOOMERANGS AND STAFFS AS WEAPONS.

AIR NOMADS

The air nomads travel the world on flying bison, like Appa, but are based at one of four main air temples: North, South, East or West. Some air nomads live in the temples. The air nomads are a peaceful people and are the most spiritually enlightened of all the nations. They were also the first people to be attacked by the Fire Nation at the beginning of the war. They have not been seen for hundreds of years and are believed to be extinct. The air nomads are closely associated with autumn.

Airbenders cannot fly. They manipulate air currents to enhance their normal movements. As a result, airbenders can jump higher, run faster and move quicker than other benders. Aang is an extremely skilled airbender. Being the Avatar means that he is the only person in the world who can also bend fire, water and earth, although his skills are not developed in these areas.

Although airbenders cannot fly, they can ride on air currents using their staffs, which transform into gliders.

FIRE NATION

UNLIKE THE AIR, EARTH AND WATER NATIONS, WHOSE PEOPLE LEAD A SIMPLE EXISTENCE, THE FIRE NATION IS IN THE MIDDLE OF AN INDUSTRIAL REVOLUTION AND HAS STEAM-POWERED TRANSPORTS TO HELP WITH TRAVEL AND MOVING SUPPLIES. IT IS THE FIRE NATION WHO IS RESPONSIBLE FOR STARTING THE WAR, BELIEVING IT IS THEY WHO SHOULD RIGHTLY DOMINATE THE WORLD. THE FIRE NATION IS CLOSELY ASSOCIATED WITH SUMMER.

ALTHOUGH FIREBENDERS LACK DEFENSIVE POWERS, THEY MAKE UP FOR THIS WITH A WIDE VARIETY OF OFFENSIVE MOVES. A QUICK JAB OR KICK PRODUCES A SHORT-RANGE BURST OF FLAME. WHIRLWIND AND SPINNING KICKS PRODUCE BLAZING ARCS AND RINGS OF FIRE THAT EXPLODE IN ALL DIRECTIONS WITH PUNCHES CREATING FIREBALLS. IF A NUMBER OF FIREBENDERS COMBINE THEIR POWER, THEY CAN CREATE MISSILES OF FLAME THAT CAN FLY OVER LONG DISTANCES WITH DEVASTATING EFFECTS. ALTHOUGH THEY POSSESS TERRIFYING POWERS, FIREBENDERS HAVE THEIR WEAKNESSES. THEIR POWER IS INFLUENCED BY THE SUN.

IF THERE IS AN ECLIPSE, THEY LOSE THEIR POWERS UNTIL THE SUN RETURNS. THEY ALSO CANNOT BEND IF THEY ARE UNDERWATER, AND THE RAIN WEAKENS THEIR POWERS. MEMBERS OF THE FIRE NATION WHO CANNOT BEND CARRY SWORDS AND SPEARS.

LITTLE IS KNOWN ABOUT THE PEOPLE OF THIS NATION OTHER THAN THEY ARE A PROUD AND STRONG PEOPLE. USING THEIR HEAVY, MUSCULAR BODIES, THEY MANIPULATE THE GROUND FOR ATTACK AND DEFENSE.

THEY CAN KNOCK AN ENEMY OFF HIS FEET BY POUNDING THE GROUND, CREATING A SMALL EARTHQUAKE. THEY CAN ALSO USE THE EARTH TO CATAPULT THEM INTO THE AIR TO AVOID ATTACKS AND CREATE FISSURES IN THE GROUND TO SWALLOW ENEMIES. OTHER MOVES INCLUDE RAISING STONE SLABS FROM THE GROUND FOR OFFENSE AND DEFENSE, AS WELL AS LEVITATING AND THROWING ROCKS.

HIGH-LEVEL EARTHBENDERS HAVE THE POWER TO TURN THE GROUND INTO QUICKSAND TO TRAP THEIR ENEMIES. EARTHBENDERS ARE ALSO ABLE TO MAGNETIZE THEIR LIMBS TO STONE, WHICH ALLOWS THEM TO CLIMB WALLS AND CLIFFS. THE EARTH KINGDOM IS CLOSELY ASSOCIATED WITH SPRING.

EARTH KINGDOM

SEE YOU NEXT TIME!

BUSTIN' OUT FROM BIKINI BOTTOM!

SPONGEBOB'S GOT HIS OWN CINE-MANGA™